FEEDING THE SPIRIT

Nancy Brady Cunningham

Resource Publications, Inc.
160 E. Virginia St., #290
San Jose, CA 95112

Editorial director: Kenneth Guentert
Production editor: Elizabeth J. Asborno
Production assistant: Lisa Kaufman
Cover design and production: Andrew Wong
Back cover photo: Denise Geddes
Illustrations on pages 15 and 21: Carol Dykas

Library of Congress Cataloging-in-Publication Data:
Cunningham, Nancy Brady, 1944-
    Feeding the spirit : how to create your own ceremonial rites,
festivals, and celebrations / by Nancy Brady Cunningham.
        p. cm.
    Bibliography: p.
    ISBN 0-89390-117-2 (pbk.) : $7.95
    1. Spiritual life. 2. Rites and ceremonies. I. Title.
BL624.C86 1988
291.4'46dc19   88-15051
                                                                         CIP

5 4 3 2

The cover and inside illustrations appear courtesy of the following:
Grafton, Carol Belanger. Treasury of Art Nouveau Design & Orna-
ment: A Pictorial Archive of 577 Illustrations. NY: Dover Publications,
Inc., 1980.

To my children, Devin and Cara, with all my love.

Contents

Introduction

Do the days, months, even years go by so quickly that you feel swept up in a tidal wave — rushing headlong into the future — with hardly a pause along the way?

Or are you someone with lots of spare time wondering how you could spend it more meaningfully?

Or perhaps you are a "spiritual" person already familiar with an inner journey and looking for a new outlet for your energies.

Many people in today's materialistic society feel that none of their myriad activities "feed their spirit" — nothing is "soul-satisfying." And so they have a disquieting feeling that some deeper component of life is missing. They are left with the nagging suspicion that something of a more substantial nature is lacking — something to give meaning to life in a personal way.

What is this magical, elusive something? Since it is different for each person, this book will help you create a quiet space in your life in which you can discover your own key to life's hidden treasures. By using very simple tools, you can follow the formulas in this book to unlock a special place in the psyche.

You can look at *Feeding the Spirit* as a collection of twenty-four recipes (all the ingredients are listed at the beginning of each one) meant to fill an inner hunger!

So put on your ceremonial robes — that is,

your contemplative attitude
your individual attention
your favorite music
your "special" clothes,

and come to the feast.

Ingredients
for a Ceremony

Necessary Ingredients

Attention

Your attention will invest the most commonplace items with power and life. Just as you focus a camera from blurry to sharp, you need to draw the mind to one point. Now concentrate on your movements and the object you are working with, blocking out any distractions.

Action

The simple act of lighting a candle can be done ceremoniously. Just pay attention to your every move, slow down your actions, and be aware of the reactions of your senses: how the grating of the match against the cover sounds, how the eyes adjust to the soft light, how the burnt match smells, and how the heat from the candle warms your face.

Attitude

Each ceremony is a unique gift you give yourself. Use a relaxation technique — such as tensing and relaxing each part of the body in turn — before you begin.

The following are other relaxation exercises you can use:

1) Lie on your back and listen to a piece of soothing music.

2) Visualize yourself in a serene setting, e.g. at the sea listening to the waves lap at the shore, as you lie on the beach soaking up the sun.

3) Count down from 10-0 slowly, telling yourself you'll relax more deeply with each number.

4) Massage your face, shoulders, and neck as you lie on your back.

5) Take deep breaths while lying flat on your back. With each inhalation puff up your abdomen and as you exhale pull the stomach muscles in tightly. Breathe in through the nose and exhale through the nose slowly. Repeat until you feel relaxed.

6) Sit up straight, with a candle flame at eye level — concentrate on the flame until you feel relaxed.

7) Lie down on your back and take ten deep breaths, each time exhaling with an audible sigh.

8) Sit up straight and take ten deep breaths, each time exhaling with the sound of the letter "M." This sound has a soothing effect on both mind and body and therefore acts as a natural tranquilizer.

9) Lying on your back, inhale and while you hold the breath tense your whole body; i.e., make fists, make a face, tighten every muscle from head to toe. Then exhale through the mouth and relax the entire body. Repeat 5-10 times, 'til you feel tension has been drained out of you.

It is important to include at least one of these relaxation exercises at the very beginning of your ceremony, so you create a gulf between your busy life and this special block of time you've allotted for your time of celebration. So assemble the ingredients, *relax*, and then begin.

Optional Ingredients

Music

Use any music that appeals to you — music for dance, music for pensive thought, music for remembering places or people, music for evoking certain feelings.

Clothing

Any garment that makes you feel special — a skirt you made, a shirt you decorated, a shawl that belonged to Gramma or a robe you set aside to be worn only at special times; i.e., a ceremonial robe.

Jewelry

Any piece that holds special memories or a piece that enhances your self-worth (its monetary worth is incidental).

Make-up

Cosmetic make-up or theatrical make-up or body paint.

Fasting

Skip the meal prior to your ceremony, or fast all day.

Washing

If you feel tired, take a shower to renew your energies before you begin your ceremony.

If you feel tense and nervous, a short soak in the tub will relax you.

Participants

Perform the ceremony alone or ask family and/or friends to join in.

Sounds

To begin and end your ceremony, ring a bell, jangle a wind chime, strike a gong, or bang a drum.

Poetry

If you include poetry, even if you are alone, read it aloud.

Art

Any pottery, sculpture, paintings, prints, or wall hangings that help to create a sacred space for your ceremony.

Sewing/Art Supplies

You can use scissors, paper, crayons, paints, yarn, sparkles, sequins, glue, feathers, shells, etc. You needn't worry about being artistic — dare to experiment!

Flowers

Place one in your hair. Arrange them in a vase. Cut off the stems and float the flowers in a bowl of water — preferably a clear, glass bowl. Entwine the stems of the flowers to make a wreath — and decorate your wreath with ribbon, lace, sequins, or whatever you have on hand.

Scents

Burn sticks of incense or burn powdered incense over charcoal. If you are allergic to incense, burn sage leaves. Or you can use essence oils — found at the health food store — by placing a few drops behind your ears or into a bowl of water, or you can anoint a candle with the oil *before* you light it.

Helpful Hints for Group Celebrations

If you are preparing a ritual for a group, here are some considerations as you plan your celebration.

First, take a long look at the physical setting. The room should be a comfortable temperature — if people are chilly, they won't be able to relax into the ritual; if they are too warm, they will be preoccupied with beating the heat. It's best to sit on a carpeted floor with a large throw pillow for each person. For those participants who find this arrangement uncomfortable, use meditation benches (available in most health food stores) that allow a person to sit close to the floor in a posture that alleviates back tension. An inexpensive alternative to meditation benches, but one that is not therapeutic for the back, is the use of sand chairs. These are generally used for the beach or backyard, and because they are only four inches off the floor, sand chairs allow the participant to be at the same level as those seated on the floor. Or if floor sitting is out for your group, use a large dining room table with everyone seated in straightback chairs. My preference is to have folks sit on the floor, as it places everyone literally on "common ground" — an instantly unifying factor for the group. Lastly the lighting needs to be soft and indirect. Overhead fluorescents are definitely out, since stark lighting harshly affects the nervous system, and the goal here is to present a setting that radiates soft, relaxed, quieting sensations so as to encourage a sharing of intimate thoughts and feelings. Candlelight is very effective in this regard.

Candles do present a slight risk, however, so be sure to have water on hand. Either place a container of water nearby or plan the celebration in a room adjoining the bathroom or kitchen. Cover all surfaces where candles will be set down with tin foil, or place burning candles on a glass or metal serving tray or even on a dinner plate. If candles are to be hand-held (in a procession, for example), cover the base of each one with a piece of tin foil creating a foil lip to catch the hot drippings. A little extra care must be taken if people are in flowing costume or wearing masks that impair their vision — in these cases use votive candles in glass containers or candlesticks surrounded by clear glass chimneys.

Choose your music carefully and pre-set cassette tapes so there'll be no awkward pauses as you rewind looking for the correct song. It's often pleasant to have instrumental music playing when people arrive so as to set the mood immediately. Listen closely to the lyrics of any vocals you use to make certain the message of the song fits well with the theme of the ritual.

When incorporating arts and crafts materials, take time beforehand to be sure that staplers work, glue bottles squirt, and magic markers are still juicy. Go through the project once to see if you've forgotten to put out some vital ingredient. To insure the continuation of the ritual mood, ask people to work on the arts and crafts project in silence, otherwise the conversation between folks turns to the mundane; also they then spend more time chatting than working on the project. To keep a meditative mood use instrumental music or a chant that everyone can sing along with as they create their work of art.

Flowers are a welcome addition to any ritual —
here are some tips for helping them last longer. At the
florist or roadside stand, look for flowers that have
clear color and firm green leaves since these are the
hallmarks of fresh flowers. When you get them home,
strip off the foliage from the parts of the stems that
will be under water, because leaves in the water will
decay and attract bacteria. Next, snip about an inch
from the bottom of the stems, *while* holding the stems
in a bowl of water. If you cut the stems in the air, the
internal pressure will suck more air in, creating air
bubbles in the vessels that will prevent the stems from
taking more water. Add a pinch or two of sugar to the
water; better still, use the commercial flower preserv-
atives available at stores, since they not only provide
sugar as food to nourish the buds, they also contain
an acidifier to help them keep their color and a bacteria retardant to keep the water clean. Keep flowers
away from drafts, direct sunlight, and warm tempera-
tures. Last of all, you can prolong the lives of your cut
flowers by putting them somewhere cool at night —
on the floor, in the garage, or even in the refrigerator
— but be careful not to let them freeze.

Next a few suggestions on making people feel comfortable, especially if they are new to the concept of
ritual. To begin ask each person to share their name
and their reason for joining the celebration. This allows folks to get to know each other a little bit. Then
tell them about yourself, why you chose to coordinate
this celebration, and, most importantly, give a brief
description of the ritual so everyone has a preview
peek. At least once more before the ceremony is over
ask for feedback from the group. For example, if
everyone's just written a regret on a piece of paper and
collectively burnt them in a clay pot, wait 'til the fire

is out and then ask if anyone wishes to share their regret with the group. Or ask if the ritual brought up painful feelings for anyone and continue by asking if someone's willing to share that painful experience with the group. If the person begins to cry, assure them they can take all the time they need and that the group will wait for them to finish. Perhaps someone in the group will hold their hand to offer non-verbal support. These heartfelt sharings often cement the group experience.

Other ways of including participants are to ask if anyone would like to share a song or a poem or a reading that's meaningful to them. Or when sending out invitations to the ceremony, ask each person to bring, for example, a special something that embodies the essence of that season. When everyone is assembled, let each person do a "show and tell" and then place their contribution in the center of the group circle, thereby creating a seasonal centerpiece that has personal meaning for each participant.

Perhaps the most important aspect of preparing for a ritual is to make certain that each individual gets at least two opportunities to share themselves with the group during the course of the celebration, so all come away from the experience feeling their unique contributions added to the group's overall appreciation of the ritual.

Jewels

Ingredients

1 candle
1 piece of jewelry that has special significance for you
music (optional)

Light a candle and sit quietly looking closely at your piece of jewelry; notice how it catches the light, see it in a new way as you examine it closely.

If you are in a group, pair off and share with your partner what this piece means to you and why. Then have your partner ceremoniously place your piece of jewelry on you.

Or use a piece of jewelry that belonged to a deceased loved one. Place it in your hands, close your eyes and think about your deceased friend or relative.

Then concentrate on one of his/her qualities you'd like to possess.

Now say to yourself something like, "This ring symbolizes my grandmother's warm generosity — as I place this ring on my finger now, let my own abundance rise up in me and overflow."

(Be aware that you are connecting with your own inner qualities in this exercise — not necessarily with the deceased.)

Dream Making

Ingredients

pencil and paper
drawing paper
crayons or
markers or
paints or
colored pencils
music
a special song like John Denver's "Poems and Prayers and
*   Promises"*

If you've ever jotted down a dream, kept a dream journal, or can now recall a dream that had an impact on you, here's your chance to work with that dream in a ceremonial way.

First write down the dream.

Then using crayons or markers or paints, draw a picture from your dream of any of the following:

of a scene in the dream
of a mood in the dream
of a person in the dream
of anything notable in the dream.

Quietly gaze at the picture for ten minutes. Use background music and candlelight here if you wish.

Then still gazing at the picture or lying down and closing your eyes,

allow the dream to unfold again, anew.
Maybe it will take the same route as before.
Maybe not.

Try not to manipulate it.
Try not to overwork it.
Let the dream speak to you in some way.
Then ask a question of the dream, or of a dream figure.
Wait for an answer.

The answer may come in any of the following forms:

words
gestures
a snatch of a piece of music
a sound
a scent
or simple silence.

Jot down your question and answer on the back of the picture.

For one week, every night at bedtime, look at your picture and read the dream message on the back.

Note if this has any effect on your dreaming that week.

Keep pencil and paper by the bed and jot down your dreams all week long.

Mask Making

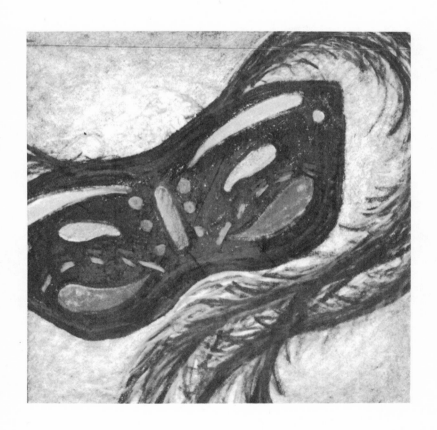

Ingredients

1 eye mask (like the Lone Ranger wore)
at least two of the following:
   paint
   markers
   feathers
   sequins
   stickers
   icicles (Christmas tree kind)
   beads
   jewelry
   any craft material
sewing supplies
glue
stapler
tape
string
scissors

Take this simple eye mask and transform it by letting your imagination run wild!

Paint it.
Spray it.
Sew on sequins.
Add jewelry.
Staple on tinsel icicles.
Glue on fake jewels.
Stick on heart-shaped stickers.
Attach feathers.
String on beads.

This can be done in a group, but ask all participants to keep conversation to a bare minimum. You might play some meditative music to help the group calm down, and in the quiet their creative juices will flow.

The mask making can be the whole ceremony culminating with folks trying on their masks. Pass around a mirror — let everyone see themselves. Then, those who wish can go to the center of the circle of participants and walk around slowly, looking directly at each of the other masked people there.

Or the mask making can be the beginning of this ceremony. Now continue the theme of the mask by using make-up or body paint to decorate other parts of the body.

If you wish to continue, you could have each person take a turn getting in the center of the circle and moving in a way that represents the essence of their mask/self. This whole process could be enhanced by playing music, so the person in the center will move/dance/crawl/skip to the music. Or since most folks are shy, rather than single turns let everyone simultaneously move to the music, interacting with each other, and moving spontaneously.

If you do this mask making alone, you may want to sit before a mirror, gazing at yourself wearing your mask. Allow yourself to sink into the feelings your mask elicits from your depths. If you wish to continue, play some appropriate music and watch yourself dance before the mirror. Then turn away and use the whole room to dance. Come back and conclude the ceremony sitting in front of the mirror once again — contemplating this newly found piece of yourself discovered through a simple mask.

Color Meditation

Ingredients

8 crayons of different colors
8 pieces of white paper
pen or pencil or marker
music (any peaceful peace; e.g., "Let It Be" by the Beatles)

Although many sources define what each color means in terms of personal qualities and in regard to which color heals which part of the body, I prefer to let people free associate.

To begin, color only one color on each piece of paper, leaving as much white space as you wish.

One at a time, gaze at the pieces of paper and spend at least one minute with each piece. End each one-minute segment by writing under each splash of color what quality that color represents to you.

Now choose a quality/color you feel in need of at this time; e.g., energy, peace, or solitude. Gaze at the piece of paper and let the color come into your being on each breath. As you sit quietly, let your breathing deepen.

As you inhale, with the eyes open, feel you are breathing in this color. Close your eyes and exhale and feel/visualize this color flooding through your body. Continue this breathing technique while listening to the music you chose.

When you are finished, put on a piece of clothing in the healing color you picked and feel yourself wrapped in the quality this color represents to you. Wear this piece of clothing for the rest of the day, or even to bed if you wish.

Ritual Bath

Ingredients

*essence oil (e.g., musk, rose, etc., available at health food
   stores)*
flowers
thirsty towel
scented massage oil or your favorite body lotion
new clothes or old favorites to slip into after the bath
*soft music (Never touch electrical equipment while in
   tub or before drying off.)*
candlelight (optional)

You can use this ceremony for the following occasions:

To celebrate a child's birthday — the whole family can
help prepare the bath.

To celebrate the onset of menses — let a mother prepare this for her daughter.

To celebrate any special day.

To give yourself a lift.

To prepare for any of the celebrations in this book.

For no reason at all.

While drawing the bath, do the following:

1) Pour in two or three drops of essence oil.

2) Take time to slowly, gently, sensuously comb your
hair or your child's hair.

When the bath is drawn,

1) Strew flowers on the water.

2) Slowly, carefully wash yourself or your child.

3) Dry off, taking your time.

4) Massage the body with oil or lotion.
5) Get dressed unhurriedly.

Perform this ritual bath in silence except for the background music. It will add to the specialness of these moments if you do not engage in conversation when others
are involved.

Dance of the
Seven Veils

Ingredients

a mirror (full length is best)
a veil (any piece of chiffon or nylon, or a light-weight shawl,
or a large scarf will do)
music — a slow instrumental piece, or a collection of your
favorite slow-tempered vocals; (e.g., "Something" by
George Harrison)

The veil represents an extension of the halo or aura around your body.

As a prelude to this ceremony, you may want to do the Ritual Bath or the Color Meditation, found elsewhere in this book.

At first, move to the music with your eyes closed.
Then, begin to dance with the veil.
Let it move like a separate entity.
Let it have a mind of its own.

You needn't try to control it or to have it move in some preconceived way.
Now use the mirror to get a glimpse of how you look.
Or if this is too inhibiting, dance with your shadow on the wall.
Since you are alone with your music, allow yourself as much freedom as possible.
Toss your veil and watch it settle down slowly by itself.

Toss it while you're moving.
Toss it when you're standing still.
Toss it high.

Toss it low.
Toss it over your shoulder.

Each time watch your veil float to the floor.

It's a bird with diaphanous wings.
It's a butterfly all a-flutter.
It's a glider silently floating to earth.
It's a kite sinking into a colorful pile.

To end this ceremony,

Place the veil over your head and face.
Sit quietly.
Let the experience wash over you.
Be aware of the texture of the material,
of the softness
of your breath
of the silence.

When you are ready, ceremoniously fold up your veil
and put it away.

Birthday
Celebration

Ingredients

a candle
a small knife
a Magic Marker
stone, leaf, or piece of wood, etc.
music (e.g., "Burn Slowly the Candle of Life" by the Moody
* Blues)*

Reflect on the season of your birth — do you enjoy this season? On a scale of 1-4, where does this season fall in your estimation? What colors do you associate with your birthday season? Choose a candle in one of these colors.

Now carve a birthday wish for the coming year on your candle. Set the candle aside; don't light it just yet.

Take a piece of natural material — a stone, a leaf, a piece of wood, etc., and write on it your main regret from the past year.

To symbolize letting go of this regret, you are going to dispose of it in a natural setting, in accordance with the season of your birth.

Fall is represented by the earth, so take your stone or leaf or piece of bark, and write on it. Then bury it in the earth if you have an autumn birthday.

We all need warmth in winter, so burn your regret, written on a piece of wood or bark or on a leaf. Use a fireplace or any safe receptacle and watch your regret go up in smoke.

Spring is a time of renewal ushered in on warm winds, so write your regret on a new leaf, tear it into confetti-like pieces and throw it to the winds.

Those of you who are summer babies, write your regret on a piece of driftwood, a corn husk, or a leaf and let the cooling waters of a brook, stream, lake, or ocean cleanse you (at least temporarily) of your regret, as you watch it sail away on summer waters.

Come indoors and light your candle. Think about your birthday wish. Imagine it coming true. When you are ready, blow out your candle and listen to the special song you chose for this part of the celebration. For the next year, once each month, relight your candle and rekindle your wish.

A Ritual of Support for a Sick Friend

Ingredients

*candles — one for each participant — light before ritual
  begins*
essence oil
a spool of brightly colored yarn or string
a large bowl of water
a glass for each participant
music

I call this a ritual of support rather than a healing ritual because healing another, in my opinion, is not within our power. But we can use this ritual to be supportive, giving of our warm vibes and gentle energies to lift our ailing friend's spirits.

And so even in the case of terminal illness, this rite can still be used, since it doesn't imply offering the false hope of a cure when none is in sight.

When faced with the impending death of a loved one, most folks feel overwhelmingly helpless. This ritual may aid in alleviating some of this feeling since it allows family and friends to gather together and *do* something. Such a tangible display of support consoles the dying patient, who will feel awash in warmth and love, knowing aloneness and abandonment will not be their lot at the end of life.

On the other hand, in the case of serious illness, when the outcome seems to be held in a delicate balance, we can use this ceremony to say: "If you get well, we'll be here to rejoice with you. If you fade we'll be here 'til you die — to the end you can rest easy in the comfort of our support."

1) To blend the energies of the group, ladle out a glass of water for each member of the group.

Now each person meditates on his/her glass of water and then breathes into it three times, letting the breath carry their healing energies into the water. Pass the glass over the lit candle to add warmth.

Everyone empties their glass into the bowl of water in the center and the leader stirs the water to mingle the energies of the group.[1]

2) Pass around a spool of brightly colored yarn. Each person wraps the yarn around his/her right wrist a couple of times and passes the spool to the next person. Let each person say something supportive to the patient as they bind their right wrist. When the whole group is bound together, sing a song like "You've Got A Friend" by Carol King, or simply play the song and let everyone listen to it. The purpose of this part of the ritual is to demonstrate graphically that the patient and the loved ones are all bound together in this illness. They are all entwined in the patient's life and are offering their support as consolation to the patient. Then pass the spool back around the group in the opposite direction, while rewinding the yarn onto the spool.

3) Pass around a bottle of essence oil. Each participant smells it and anoints some part of their body with a drop of oil. When all have had a turn, the leader pours a few drops of oil into the bowl of water in the center of the circle.

4) Each person now takes a turn anointing the sick person with the energized, scented water. Dip two fingers into the water and place them on the ailing area of your friend's body.

At the same time say, "I anoint you with my ... (name a strength you have that you wish to bestow on your friend)."

5) Play some background music and let each person take a turn giving their friend a hug and a kiss and saying something personal that's for their friend's ears only — a private sharing not shared with the group.

6) End with a song everyone knows, for example "Perhaps Love" by John Denver. The leader can conclude this ritual with a quote, such as, "Your sunshine smiles on the winter days of my heart, never doubting it's spring flowers" (Tagore).

NOTES

1. Adapted from "The Water Ceremony" in *Earth Rites*, Vol. 2 of *Rituals* by Sherry Mestel, 82.

Tree Meditation

Ingredients

a bird house
bird feed, such as sunflower seeds
a poem about a tree

Choose a tree — one on your property or in a quiet woods where you or your group will not be disturbed.

1) Lie down under the tree with bare feet against the trunk and outstretched arms touching the people beside you. If you are working in a group, the tree trunk will be the hub of a wheel with each person representing a spoke and the circle of outstretched arms forming the wheel's rim.

2) In silence stare up at the sky *through* the branches of the tree. Notice the pattern formed by the branches darkly outlined against the pale sky. Be aware of the dappled sunlight pouring down through the leaves. Follow the clouds on their airy journey as they dart by or lazily roll about the sky.

3) Deeply relax by taking ten deep breaths — on each inhalation feel the life of the tree traveling into your body through the soles of your bare feet. As you exhale let go of all tension. After the tenth breath, lie there in silence, totally relaxed for 2-10 minutes.

4) Now stand and, if in a group, form a circle around the tree without joining hands. Close the eyes. Stretch up and imagine

your arms are the tree's branches
your fingers the leaves
your skin the bark
your blood the sap
your legs the trunk
your bare feet the growing roots that extend down
    into the ground.

5) Feel a genuine connection with earth through this root system. Feel centered, grounded, earthy. Keeping the eyes closed, begin to move hands, arms, and upper body like a tree swaying in the wind, while reciting the following short verse aloud:

The wind she lifts my laughter
The wind she lifts my cares
And bearing both my pain and joy
She thus my body bears.[1]

6) Since trees provide shelter and food for birds, you or your group can now make an offering to these feathered friends.

Hang a birdhouse in the tree (perhaps one the group all had a hand in creating); or
Hang bags of suet from the branches; or
Hang pine cones that are suspended by a string. First slather the cone with peanut butter and then roll it in sunflower seeds; or
Use bread crusts — hang each one from a brightly colored ribbon or piece of yarn; or ...
If the tree is too tall, pass around a bag of sunflower seeds, giving each person a turn to scoop out a handful and sprinkle them on the ground under the tree.
7) End with someone reading a poem about a tree.

NOTES

1. Gearhart, *The Wanderground*, 104.

House Blessing

Ingredients

white candles in candleholders for each participant

rosemary, fresh from your herb garden or from the grocery store. (Dried, chopped rosemary is on the spice aisle; If you want it fresh, look on the produce aisles.)

salt, just a pinch to be added to the large bowl of water

fresh flowers in each room of the house or bouquet in the central room where this ritual will take place

plastic cups for each person

incense

large bowl of water and a ladle or a large serving spoon

a large goblet of wine

music: "'Tis a Gift to be Simple," a traditional folk song from the recording called Many Blessings *by* On Wings of Song

This ceremony can be used in any of the following situations:

As a prelude to a housewarming party.

To christen a new office.

To "clear the air" as you move into a recently vacated house, apartment, or condominium.

To anoint a room in your home that you've just re-decorated.

To celebrate the culmination of spring or fall housecleaning.

Anytime you want to change the vibrations in a room or in your home.

1) To begin, light the incense.

2) From a central white candle, each person lights an individual white candle to symbolize purity.

3) Play a recording of music that suggests new beginnings — perhaps "Rites of Spring" by Stravinsky.

4) As the music plays, form a procession and walk through each room in the house.[1] As the group comes to a room, the homeowner shuts off the lights in that room and the group walks through the room with their lit candles. This act represents bringing "a new light of purity" to every room in the house. Everyone in the procession keeps silent. If the music is on cassette, ask one guest to carry the recorder from room to room, so wherever you go in the house the music travels with you. If this isn't possible, turn the volume up on the stereo before beginning the procession, so the music is audible throughout the house.

5) Return to the room where the procession originated.

6) Sit in a circle around the bowl of water — use something festive, like a punch bowl.

7) Each person adds a pinch of salt to the water. Since salt is a purifying agent, each guest makes a wish for the homeowner that has something to do with purity. For example, one might wish that all who reside in the home be blessed with purity of heart, while another wishes that the owner be blessed with a maid to keep the house as sparkling clean as it looks presently.

8) Each guest now takes a turn adding a sprinkle of rosemary to the water. Rosemary is an herb that traditionally symbolizes protection. Each person takes a turn wishing the home be protected from negative forces ranging from robbers to household arguments.

9) The homeowner stirs the water, blending a personal mixture of purity and protection for the new home and symbolically mingling all the good wishes from the group.

10) Ladle out a cup of this water for each person. The guests then take their cups and white candles and go outside. Singing "Tis a Gift to be Simple," the group walks around the house sprinkling purifying water on the foundation. Continue singing as all gather indoors.

11) Conclude with each toasting the homeowner and taking a sip of wine from the goblet as an expression of good will toward all who will inhabit this new space.

NOTES

1. Guentert, ed., *Winter Festivals*, 98.

A
Contemplative Day

The next four celebrations — one for sunrise, noontime, twilight, and night — can be used together to form
the framework of a contemplative day spent with friends
and family.

This day could also be part of a weekend or weeklong
retreat. Silence can be requested for the whole day or just
part of it. Spending silent time with others gives rise to a
deep awareness of each other.

Sunrise Ceremony

Ingredients

candle (in a sun color: orange, yellow, gold, or red) for
  each person
candleholders
decorate the room (optional) with flowers in yellow, red, and
  orange
music, a sun song (e.g., "Here Comes the Sun" by the Beatles)
a poem, story, or myth about the sun
a bell, gong, or wind chime

1) Sit in the darkness before the first streak of dawn. Each person lights a candle, while sitting in a circle, thereby creating a fiery sphere representing the sun. (If outdoors, use votive candles protected from the wind by glass containers.)

2) The leader reads a sun poem or story or myth. The children's library abounds with such stories; for example, you can easily find simplified versions of myths concerning Re or Icarus or Helius there. If the leader would like to relax during this part, then tape the reading in advance.

3) As the sky begins to lighten with the first streaks of dawn, sing the Beatles' "Here Comes the Sun" or some other sun song. Pass out lyrics so all can join in.

4) As first rays of sunlight appear (*before* the sun itself is actually seen), each person heralds the imminent arrival of the sun by taking turns striking a gong, ringing a bell, or jangling a wind chime.

5) When the sun first peeks over the horizon (before it is completely visible), greet the sun with a group mantra;

i.e., recite in unison many times a single sentence, such as "Faith is the bird that feels the light and sings when the dawn is still dark" (Tagore); or "All evil vanishes from life for he who keeps the sun in his heart," an ancient Sanskrit mantra.

6) Once the sun is completely up over the horizon, the group mimics flowers opening to the morning sun. Each person moves from a crouched position through various poses to an upright stance, facing the sun with outstretched arms to receive its rays. Appropriate music can be used here to inspire each flower's growth.

Noontime
Food Blessing

Ingredients

bread
cutting board and knife
wine
wine glass for each person
one large wine goblet
other lunch foods (optional)

A meal shared in silence bestows a special blessing on the participants. This is a simple "bread, wine, and thou" affair.

1) Sit in a circle, outdoors if possible, with a loaf of bread and one large goblet of wine in the center. Everyone silently contemplates this simple fare.

2) The leader holds the bread up to the sun, aware of the part the sun played in the growing of the grain,

warming the ground in spring so the frozen earth of winter softens to receive the seeds

shining on the sprouts as they spring through the fertile soil

helping these sprouts mature 'til they are ready for harvest.

3) Leader cuts off the end crust, walks away from the group to the nearest tree, crumples the crust and scatters the crumbs beneath the tree as a gift for the birds.

4) Returning to the group, the leader ceremoniously pours some of the wine onto the ground as an offering to Mother Earth, who nurtured the vines on which the grapes grew.

5) Now the loaf is passed around the circle in a counter-clockwise direction, while each person takes a turn tearing off a chunk of bread, makes eye contact with the person to the right, and passes the remainder of the loaf to that person.

6) Now the glass of wine is passed; each takes a sip and makes eye contact as the goblet is passed from person to person.

7) When done, all hold hands, close eyes, and silently appreciate the feeling of community, the sunshine, the taste of bread and wine.

8) To conclude, everyone can break out other foods to share — either continuing in silence or sharing conversation during this part of the meal.

9) Rest, relax, or nap in the sun as a group after lunch.

Twilight Candles

Ingredients

a sunset
one candle for each person in any shade of blue, purple or gray
    to represent the colors of dusk
candle holders for each candle
one bright yellow or vibrant orange candle to represent the sun
music — perhaps something classical

Twilight is a magical time — neither day nor night. The busyness of the day is behind us and the evening meal or activity is not yet underway. It's a time for pensive thought and, for some, a time of sadness and longing.

1) Watch the sunset as a group.

2) Just at the moment when the sun slips below the horizon, each person lights a candle from the central, sun candle, symbolizing the extension of the sun's light and energy and warmth.

3) Sit silently in the gathering dusk, noting the changing colors of the sky as the day fades and finally dies. Here play some appropriate music — perhaps excerpts from "Pathetique" by Tchaikovsky or Mozart's "Requiem Mass."

4) When there's not a trace of color left in the sky, everyone takes a candle and forms a circle; then slowly the group walks in a circle representing the movement of the cycle of the day. Continue playing music for this part. No electrical lighting is used in the room, for it has a disquieting effect on the nervous system. Candlelight elicits a calm, introspective feeling from people, so use only

candles to illumine the room. As folks move in this slow circular walk, be aware that the day's cycle has ended but the night's cycle has just begun.

5) Now each person breaks from the circle and does a short candle dance — simply moving to the music and incorporating the candle. Note the shadows thrown by the dancing figure and his/her candle. Each person has a turn; then sit again in a group and break the silence for the first time since this ritual began. Let each person share their thoughts and feelings about this experience before ending.

Starshine

Ingredients

a candle in a nighttime color:
  a) the gray of clouds as they scoot in front of the moon
  b) deep indigo blue of the midnight sky
  c) the silver twinkling of the stars
  d) the pale yellow or white of the moon
  e) black the absence of light, the color of night
a candleholder
music: "Starborn Suite" by Steve Halpern and "When You
  Wish Upon a Star" by Linda Ronstadt
star-shaped stickers
stick of incense or sparkler for each person
tin foil and scissors for each person
spool of very thin string
Scotch tape

1) Sit together in a room illuminated only by candlelight.

2) Pass around a stick of incense or a sparkler. Each person uses it to draw a star in the air, making a silent or verbal wish upon this star as it is drawn. Meanwhile the rest of the group keeps up the following constant chant:

"Star light, star bright — first star I see tonight. I wish I may, I wish I might, have this wish I wish tonight."

3) Each participant keeps his/her wish in mind as the group leader places a star sticker on the person's face. As this is being done, the group addresses the person receiving the star, saying, for example, "Pam, may your wish come true."

4) Let the group decide on a wish for something important to the group as a whole.

5) While listening to "Starborn Suite," each cuts out a few tin foil stars and ties a long string to each star, all the while contemplating the group's wish.

6) The group leader tapes these strings to the ceiling so that the stars are suspended. The group stands, joins hands, and sings "When You Wish Upon a Star" three times. Leave the stars suspended for the rest of the evening as evidence of the group's wish for some common goal.

Creating
Sacred Space

Ingredients

a clay object you've either bought or created yourself; for example,
   a sun dial
   a wind chime
   a flower pot
   a bas relief
   a piece of sculpture
   a bowl
   a vase
   a bird bath
   a statue
   a planter
a private outdoor spot on your property:
   the yard
   garden
   waterfront
   back entrance to your house
   or a wooded area
a flat of flowers ready for planting
a spade
a watering can filled with water
a recording of "Turn, Turn, Turn" by the Byrds

There's a special reason why the central object in this ceremony is made of clay. The creation of any clay object incorporates the four elements: clay is composed of earth and is mixed with water in the molding process. Then, once formed, the clay piece is left to dry in the air. Finally, it is fired in the kiln; although today many potters use electric kilns rather than woodburning ones, the intense heat that is generated still represents the element of fire.

1) Bring your clay piece to a private spot on your property. Place it in different locations until. you find the perfect site for it.

2) Contemplate your clay object and the healing powers of the four elements it represents: water cleanses; fire burns out impurities; air blows away staleness and leaves a clean, fresh scent; and earth holds the secret of new growth.

3) This clay object will constantly be in contact with these elemental forces of nature since it will continuously be outdoors. It will be caressed by the winds, warmed by the sun, washed clean by the soft rains and forever in touch with the earth. Meditate for a few moments on how it would physically feel to be always open to the changing forces of sunlight, moonlight, and starlight and to directly experience the changing of the seasons as an indicator of the movement of time.

This lump of clay will manifest your desire for a simple tie to the forces of nature — that's the reason for placing it outdoors. It will connect with the healing forces of the natural world in a way you cannot. In our busy, hi-tech lives we often lose this link with living in harmony with nature.

4) Anoint this clay piece with water from the watering can.

5) With your eyes open, turn completely around three times. Do this slowly so all the visual input from your sacred space filters in. By turning around like this, you give homage to the circular path the moon and the earth and the seasons follow and to the circular shape of sun, moon, and earth.

6) As you turn 'round, sing "Turn, Turn, Turn" by the Byrds or listen to a recording of this song.

7) Plant the flat of flowers near the clay piece. Contemplate how these flowers are in sync with a larger, natural cycle as they grow, change, decay, and die. Give thought to your own life changes and unavoidable death. Modern life attempts to obliterate the rhythms of nature by forcing life into an artificial, straight-line pattern rather than merging with the natural, circular flow of the universe. Good health comes from an intimate connection with the cyclical flow of energy through and around us. This is where the importance of your clay object comes in. It is your touchstone with nature, even when you are not there. It stands serene and calm, while you dash hither and yon drowning in your busy schedule and hectic lifestyle.

8) Meditate on these thoughts awhile and then, knowing you can return at any time, prepare to take leave of your sacred space. In the future when you feel drained or hassled, return to this spot to be renewed.

Moon Magic

Ingredients

full moon
music (e.g., "Moon Circles" by Kay Gardner or "Moon Shadow" by Cat Stevens)
various props are needed depending on which month it is — refer to text for specifics
a candle in a moon color — white, silver, blue-white, pale yellow
a candlestick holder — silver if available
wear silver, pale yellow, or white clothes to represent moonlight

Our ancestors were extremely familiar with the moon in all its phases. Some positive aspects of the full moon are that it is rumored to bring good luck, wisdom, abundance, and an increase in energy. Just as the moon moves from a thin crescent to brilliant fullness and then shrinks to nothingness again, so too do we grow and change as we move through life's cycles.

Begin by turning off all the lights — sit in the moonlight (outdoors if weather permits). Light one candle and play appropriate music. The body of this active meditation varies according to the month.

January: Crystal Moon Take a crystal and begin by washing it in a cup of water to which has been added a pinch of salt. Dry the crystal gently with a piece of soft fabric. Hold the crystal over the candle flame, moving it back and forth meditatively and notice how it sparkles in the light.

February: Maiden Moon A time of new beginnings. By candlelight write down a new idea or creative project you want to see completed by the end of the year. Use a pen that writes with silver ink, if possible. Be specific — include the details of your concept. Picture your new idea as an accomplished fact — see it fully implemented as you let your imagination paint pictures in your mind's eye.

March: Spring Waters Moon Use two large bowls filled three-quarters full with room temperature water. Close your eyes, then dip your hands into the bowl, gradually extract them, and dry them with a soft towel. Next slowly dip your face into the second bowl — stay under for a few seconds — then dry off and sit quietly for five minutes,[1] feeling cleansed and ready for spring.

April: Planting Moon Meditatively plant a bulb or seed in a flower pot and ceremoniously give the impregnated soil its first drink. Close your eyes and envision yourself as the seed or bulb, bursting with life force and anticipate how you'll dazzle the world with your beauty when you finally flower.

May: The Flower Moon So named for May's abundance of colorful flowers. Arrange a bouquet of flowers in a vase of water. Take your time. Be artistic — try various combinations. Or entwine the stems of the flowers to make a May wreath and float it in a bowl of water or place it on your head.

June: The Rose Moon is next! Gaze at a rose for a few minutes, then close your eyes and try to picture it exactly. Open your eyes and see how close your mental image came to the real flower. Repeat this exercise several times.

July: Thunder Moon Strong storms fill the sky! Use a small drum, even a toy drum, and experiment with different sounds. Use drum sticks or just your hands or fingers. Imitate the rolling, menacing sounds of thunder as well as the electrifying sharp cracks and the booming thuds when the thunder is overhead.

August: Corn Moon Use some maize or Indian corn — the kind used to decorate the outside door in autumn. Hold it over the candle flame, noting the colors, texture and shape of it. Be aware of the shadow it forms on the opposite wall. Close your eyes and feel the husks and kernels, realizing you experience the corn differently using touch rather than sight — a way of seeing with your hands.

September: Harvest Moon

Take an apple.
Sensitively wash and polish it.
Notice its shape from different angles.
Close your eyes.
Feel its smooth skin.
Smell it.
Open eyes and look at it again.
Close eyes and take a bite.
Slowly chew and swallow — savor the taste.
Finish eating apple in the same way.[2]

October: Falling Leaf Moon Beforehand, gather together some colorful fall leaves, clear nail polish, and a large bowl of water.

In a slow, careful way, choose one leaf from the bunch — the one that appeals to you the most. It may be its size, shape, color, or tree of origin that makes it your favorite. Now paint this leaf, front and back, with clear nail polish to preserve it.

Take the rest of the leaves and float them in a bowl of water. Breathe on them and watch them move and dance on the water's surface. Feel the beauty of autumn filling your spirit.

November: Big Winter Moon Winter is the time when we are drawn inward. To further this inclination, sit before a mirror and study your face as a curious stranger might look at it. Rather than looking for cosmetic flaws, search your countenance to see what of your character is written there. Take as long as you like. Center now on your eyes, taking time to let them tell the tale of the happenings within.

December: Long Night Moon During the time of the winter solstice in late December occurs the longest night of the year. Remember, as the nights grow longer, the hours of moonlight increase, so December has more moonlight than any other month.

Using black construction paper, crayons, markers, glue, sparkling bits of silver paper or fabric, silver stickers, silver sequins, and Christmas tree icicles, create a moonscape, as you sit in the moonlight working by candlelight.[3]

NOTES

1. Gunther, *What To Do Til The Messiah Comes.*

2. Ibid.

3. The various names corresponding to the full moon for each month originate from *Lunatics Calendar* by Saiyda Stone (which is no longer published). The only exception is the title given to the full moon of May — that name came from *Festivals* 5, no. 2(1986):26, Resource Publications, Inc., 160 E. Virginia St., No. 290, San Jose, CA 95112.

Winter Solstice Celebration (December 20-23)

Ingredients

a candle for each participant
a mirror
gold sparkles
wine (optional, can use grape juice)
a decorative bowl half-full of water
flowers (optional — for decoration only)
gold stickers (stars, hearts, etc.)
essence oil (any scent)

The winter solstice celebrates the birth of the sun. It is also a time of darkness, however, because the sun is at its lowest point in the southern sky, thus creating the longest night of the year. Ancients referred to this phenomenon as the passing of the light, the death of the sun.

But, since from this night on the days grow longer (albeit at first only by seconds), the winter solstice heralds the birth of the new light.

So on the night of this winter celebration, the forces of light and dark struggle against each other, waging a war that you can participate in through this ceremony.

On this ominous night, the sun appears to be dying — slowly losing the fight against the encroaching darkness. This is a serious battle — without the sun there is no warmth, no light, no crops, no growth of any kind. People would quickly perish in a world forever sunless.

Darkness plays a role in the human quest for emotional balance, so we begin our tribute to this longest night of the year by honoring the dark times in our lives.

Everyone is seated in a circle in a room lit only by one candle in front of each person, and by one central candle in the center of the circle representing the sun. Silently, or aloud, each person names a loss they've experienced during the past year and blows out their candle. The group leader then takes the central candle, representing the sun, and leaves the room — representing the loss of light in our inner and outer worlds. These folks are now left in total darkness to dwell on their loss (appropriate background music can be used here). After a two- to five-minute interval, the leader returns with the sun candle, symbolizing the birth of the sun.[1]

Now everyone assists the newborn sun in its battle against the darkness.

1. Each relights his/her candle, expressing a personal hope for the coming year.

2. Each one heavily sprinkles the gold sparkles on the surface of the water in the bowl (which is in the center of the circle). As each person takes a turn sprinkling, the group chants in unison: "The seasons turn, we bring the light, we raise the sun from the dark of night."[2]

3. Place the candles close to the bowl of water. There's a magical effect created by this crust of gold sparkles moving on the surface of the water, illuminated by candelight.

4. Sing a sun song, such as "Here Comes the Sun" by the Beatles. Pass out copies of the lyrics, so everyone can join in.

5. Pass around a glass of wine. Let each person take a sip and toast the sun.

6. Leader places a few drops of essence oil in the bowl of water and then anoints every person with sunshine by dipping her hand into the scented, sparkling water and sprinklng it over the person's hair. Nice effect!

7. Each person adorns his/her face with little gold stickers. Then pass the mirror around so everyone can see how they look. It's very festive to see everyone sparkling like the sun.

NOTES

1. Cole and Ebenreck, *Sun Reflections*, 68.
2. Starhawk, *The Spiral Dance*, 170.

Candlemas Celebration (February 2)

Ingredients

a white candle for each participant
a colored candle for each of the four compass points. See text
    for color selection that corresponds with each direction.
optional: four posters representing each of the four times of
    the day — sunrise, noontime, twilight, and midnight, or
    use a poster for each of the four seasons.

As the winter months drag on, the festival of Candlemas is celebrated to "lighten" our load. This is a celebration of the ever-increasing amount of daylight at this time of the year. At the end of December when we celebrate the winter solstice, it is dark by 4:30 in the afternoon. Just six weeks later at the beginning of February, we have gained almost an hour more of daylight; at Candlemas, then, we acknowledge the additional daylight and its inherent promise that spring is waiting in the wings. Traditionally Candlemas is also a time for purification and healing, so this ritual includes both.

Different healing energies come from the four directions: East heals the mind, South the spirit, West the emotions, and North the body. Each of these directions also corresponds to a particular time of day, to certain colors, to each of the four elements, and to the four seasons.

Let's begin by mapping out the room, using a compass to determine the directions if need be.

1) East corresponds to the dawn, so light a candle in a dawn color — light blue, crimson, white, or yellow — and place it in the east corner of the room. East is also re-

presented by the element air, which corresponds to the mind and mental healing, and to Spring.

2) South corresponds to noon, so light a candle in a noontime color — orange, gold, red, or crimson — and place it to the south. South is also represented by the element fire, which corresponds to the energy of the spirit, spiritual healing, and to Summer.

3) West corresponds to twilight or dusk, so light a candle in a twilight color — blue, blue-green, gray, or indigo — and place it to the west. West is represented by the element water, which corresponds to the emotions, to emotional healing, and to Autumn.

4) North corresponds to midnight so light a candle in black, brown, green or white in the northern portion of the room. North is also represented by the element earth, which corresponds to the body and to physical healing,[1] and to Winter.

5) Put up posters if you have them: sunrise to the east, noon to the south, twilight to the west, and midnight to the north; or the four seasons posters can be used.

6) Decide which aspect of your being is most in need of healing. For example, if you need emotional healing, bring your unlit white candle to the west. Let the color of the candle (and of the poster if you're using them) wash over you. Breathe in deeply three times, inhaling healing energy from the west, pulling in the color of twilight with your breath. Light your candle from this west candle; return to sit in the middle of the room, placing your candle in front of you.

7) If working in a group, let each person take a turn or the leader can ask that all needing healing of the mind go to the east and give them directions about breathing in the colors of dawn. When they return to the circle, move on to the next compass point until all four directions are done and each person has gone to one of the four directions.

8) With all candles burning in the center of the room, contemplate the fact that primitives lit bonfires in the belief that they were actually increasing the heat and energy of the sun. Feel that this collection of lit candles has the same effect at this Candlemas celebration — at a time of year when the heat and energy of the sun *are* increasing as the daylight lengthens.

9) To end this Candlemas celebration, sing or recite the lyrics to this traditional song, using it as a rite of purification:

> May the longtime sun shine upon you
> All love surround you
> And the pure light within you
> Guide your way on.

NOTES

1. Starhawk, *The Spiral Dance*, 201-3.

Spring Equinox Celebration (March 20-30)

Ingredients

potting soil
candles
small flower pots
seeds (e.g., marigold)
bowl of water
music (e.g., "Morning Has Broken" by Cat Stevens)
large spoon
a ladle

The equinoxes are times of balance because day and night are now of equal length. Since the birth of the sun at the winter solstice, the sun has grown stronger day by day until it is equal in strength and endurance to the dark forces of night. From now 'til the summer solstice, the light reigns supreme over the dark, which means there are more daytime hours than nightime ones.

This is the time of spring's return!

As the sun grows in strength, it warms the earth. This rise in the temperature of the soil encourages the seeds to germinate. The tiny sprouts reach for the sun, and the earth bursts forth in her colorful, fragrant raiment. Now is the time to joyfully celebrate life, for winter's death grip is broken.

We'll honor this time of year with a planting ceremony. First, slowly, deliberately light a candle while some appropriately springy music plays in the background. Second, if you are doing this outdoors, simply listen to the music with eyes closed as you bask in the sun. Third, place some seeds in the pot in which you've put some potting soil. Then cover the seeds with more soil.

Now give tribute to the four elements — all of which are needed to bring your seeds to life: earth, water, air, and fire. Honor the earth by patting down the soil. Acknowledge the water by scooping out a ladle of water and giving your seed a drink. Emulate spring's warm air by breathing out three times onto your plant. If you are indoors, hold your plant over the candle flame to warm the soil. If outdoors, hold the plant up to the fiery sun.

In time, your seed will poke up through the dark soil, to be bathed in spring sunshine, to quench its thirst with gentle rain, and to sway in soft breezes.

May Day (May 1)

Ingredients

an offering that embodies the scent of May (see text for examples)
two candles and candleholders
a large, decorative tray or serving platter
music (e.g., Sun Singer *by* Paul Winter *Consort)*
a vase of flowers or a flowering plant
a Polaroid camera (optional)

May is the month when the world births itself. The blustering March wind and a rainy April give rise to a riot of color and scent as the earth explodes in a floral fireworks.

Everyone is asked to bring to the group something that breathes the *scent* of May, for example,

fresh lawn clippings
a small bag of moist earth
fresh, fragrant flowers
a stick of incense in a floral scent
an essence oil in a floral scent
a pleasant smelling herb, like mint
fresh fruit

1) Sit in a circle with two lit candles, the flowers, and the tray in the center.

2) Each person takes a turn passing around his/her gift of fragrance until everyone in the circle has taken a whiff. When the gift returns to the giver, he/she

shares with the group why this scent embodies May, and then slowly, ceremoniously places this offering on the tray in the center of the circle.

3) When all have had a turn, hold hands, close eyes and do a group breath meditation:

a) Inhale deeply three times, each time exhaling with an audible sigh to relax the emotions. Inhale the greening fields and warm sun of May; exhale winter staleness. Inhale warm relaxation; exhale emotional stress. Inhale positive emotions; exhale the negative.

b) Inhale — tighten all the muscles, tense the whole body; exhale and completely relax; repeat three times. Inhale the energy of spring; exhale winter's fatigue. Inhale the open blue sky of May; exhale the confinement of winter. Inhale the physical "aliveness" of Spring; exhale bodily tension.

c) Inhale three times, slowly and deeply. Each time exhale with the sound of the letter "M." This sound has a tranquilizing effect on the mind. Inhale the serenity of spring; exhale mental tension. Inhale the tranquillity of spring flowers; exhale worry. Inhale the beauty of a world renewed in May; exhale mental confusion and anxiety.

4) Remain in a circle for a five-minute interlude during which the group keeps silent, listening to some music and letting the scents of May waft over them — with the eyes still closed so the visual input is eliminated, thereby accenting the sense of smell.

5) Open the eyes and feast them on the collection of gifts on the platter in the center of the circle. See the collection as a whole — as an abstract piece of art — as a spontaneous visual creation in honor of May Day. The leader could then carefully bring this platter to the dinner table, as a centerpiece that will grace the table during a potluck dinner or a simple sharing of

cake and wine. If possible take a Polaroid shot of the centerpiece for each participant, so each will carry home a memento of the celebration.

Summer Solstice Celebration (June 20-23)

SVMMER

Ingredients

a crystal
a rose
a bowl of water
essence oil (preferably rose)
flowers
shells
vines
twigs
corn silk
strips of corn husk
branches or any other natural elements that could be woven into a braid
strong cord suitable for braiding
music (e.g., "The Rose" by Bette Midler)

The Summer Solstice is the longest day of the year, thus the night is short and weak in comparison. Light triumphs over darkness! But victory is short-lived. The light begins to wane the very next day. We need not lose heart, though, for there will be more daylight than nighttime until the fall equinox occurs — lots of warm summer sun to keep our spirits high.

We'll celebrate this birth of summer with a purification ceremony so we can feel that we shine like the sun.

1. Anoint yourself (or your partner) with rose oil: forehead, ears, hands, and heart.

2. Bathe your face with the water from the bowl by splashing some water on the face. Take turns if working in a group.

3. If you're outdoors, each person can wade into a stream or lake on the ocean and splash water all over the body, and then return to sit in the circle.

4. Each person braids some lengths of cord, weaving into the braid some shells, twigs, wild flowers, leaves — anything that represents summer. This symbolizes weaving into your life the elements of an eternal summer. Depending on the length of the finished braid, you've created a necklace, a headband, an anklet, a bracelet, or a belt.[1] Wear your creation for the rest of this celebration.

5. Hold a crystal up to the light — do this slowly, meditatively, noticing the dancing rainbows it creates. Pass the crystal around the circle to each person. The whole group can sing John Lennon's "We All Shine On (Like the Moon and the Stars and the Sun!)," while the crystal moves from person to person.

6. Listen to "The Rose" by Bette Midler while everyone quietly gazes at the rose in the center of the circle.

NOTES

1. Starhawk, *The Spiral Dance,* 180.

Corn Celebration (August 1)

Ingredients

an unhusked ear of corn
one corn husk for each participant
a black magic marker for each person
cornmeal
large clay pot
matches
wine and one large wine glass
corn bread

Corn is the American grain. It was the staple of tribes not only in North America but also in Central America. "Corn is the ultimate symbol of fertility and life."[1]

We celebrate on August 1 the beginning of the harvest in all its abundance. The summer season is at its mid-point, and we all begin this "vacation" time with myriad plans for activities for which we don't have time during the rest of the year. This pause at the beginning of August gives us space to reflect and question: "How can we harvest our summer dreams before Labor Day is upon us?"

This ritual will help us materialize our fantasies about this particular summer and its opportunities to relax and enjoy.

1) Form a circle outdoors. An ear of corn is passed ceremoniously from person to person. All contemplate the process by which corn grows: a seed is planted in fertile Mother Earth and watered 'til a little green spout appears. The sprout matures in the sun and the rain, and ultimately it grows as tall or taller than many of us.

Within the stalks an ear of corn is revealed — a food that can sustain life. When we take the time to view growing corn in this way, it seems almost magical, and a simple ear of corn becomes a source of wonder and awe.

2) Once the corn has passed around the circle, the leader places it in the center on a decorative plate or tray.

3) Everyone lies down in a circle and joins hands. The leader takes a box of cornmeal and walks around the outside of this human circle, sprinkling cornmeal on the ground to form a yellow circle around the whole group. As he finishes drawing this cornmeal circle, he recites the following quotation by T.S. Eliot:

> "We shall not cease from exploration
> And the end of all our exploring
> Will be to arrive where we started
> And to know the place for the first time."

4) The leader reads the following meditation while everyone in the circle closes their eyes and sinks into a oneness with Mother Earth:

> Imagine you are this glorious planet — you are the Earth Mother herself.
> The mountains and hills are the curves of your body.
> The rocks form your muscles, the source of your bodily strength.
> The streams and rivers are your clear blood flowing through your body.
> The earth's soil is your fertile innards.
> The plants spring forth from your skin — feel the plants as a part of you.
> The trees are your crowning glory — birds nest in your hair.
> Animals and people roam over your body. You are at peace in a state of oneness with all living things.[2]

Lie there in the silence for five minutes, feeling the earth beneath your body — slowly coming back to an awareness of your normal bodily proportions. When you are ready, come up to a sitting position.

5) Sit in a circle; the leader passes a corn husk to each. Write on it a summer regret concerning something you had planned to do this summer but haven't.

Everyone places their regret in a large clay pot in the center of the circle. The leader ceremoniously strikes a match and lights the corn husks. As all watch their summer regrets go up in smoke, the group says in unison, "These flames burn away our regrets," repeating this chant until the fire dies out. While this part of the ceremony is being performed, each individual may feel a "freeing up" of his/her energy and may see a way to make his/her summer dream a reality on a particular upcoming day in August. Often folks spend so much energy complaining about not having the time or money to cut loose and enjoy the summer, they have little energy left to plan any fun activities. In this ritual we turn that pattern inside-out by symbolically destroying regret, a worthless obstacle to action, and thus freeing ourselves to be able to act.

6) The leader ceremoniously husks the ear of corn that has been in the center of the circle, noting that the corn begins to die the moment it is reaped. The cycles of nature feed on life that new life may come into existence. Since the summer solstice, the longest day of the year, the light has been diminishing — the days grow shorter, summer is passing.

Here everyone reflects on the reality that we are moving toward winter and makes a silent promise to make the most of the one remaining month of summer.

7) Pass around a cup of wine — everyone takes a sip and makes a toast to summer, perhaps mentioning their plans for August that they now feel free to carry out after performing this ritual, which unblocked their pent-up energies singly focused onto their regrets.

8) All feast on corn bread and wine.

NOTES

1. Mestel, ed., *Earth Rites,* 32.
2. Adapted from "Earth Meditation" in *Meditating With Children* by Deborah Rozman, 49.

Fall Equinox Celebration (September 20-23)

AUTUMN

Ingredients

a candle (in your favorite fall color)
essence oil (any scent)
music, (e.g., "Midnight [Minuet]" by Susan Osborn and John
*   Guth, from The Paul Winter Consort's album,* Common
*   Ground*
decorate the room (optional) with any of the following:
*   pumpkins*
*   gourds*
*   fall leaves*
*   fall fruits*
*   milkweed pods*
*   dried grasses*

The fall equinox is a time of exquisite balance in the cosmos. The pause between summer and fall is a bittersweet time. The forces of light are again equal with the forces of darkness. Night and day are of equal length, so we may use this time to contemplate our own inner balance in life and what factors contribute to our feelings of equilibrium. Bring to mind an activity that makes you feel centered, such as a walk in the woods or an afternoon spent listening to classical music, and focus on that activity as we celebrate the fall equinox with a candle-lighting ceremony.

1. Anoint the candle with essence oil.
2. Place a drop of oil in the center of your forehead.
3. Light the candle and sit quietly. The candle represents your commitment to keep your balance even as the days grow shorter after the fall equinox. From now 'til

the spring equinox in March, the nights will be longer than the days. Light your candle with respect for nature's cycles and see it as a beacon to illumine your way through a dark winter.

4. Listen to "Midnight" or some other appropriate music as you continue to gaze at the candle.

5. Close your eyes and visualize the activity of balance you thought about earlier — make a promise to yourself to indulge more often in such centering activities.

6. Still keeping the eyes closed, hum the sound of the letter "M" — it has a balancing effect on both body and mind.

7. Walk around the room with the candle — protect the flame with your hand so it won't blow out; this protection symbolizes caring for the activities of balance you've decided to incorporate more frequently into your life.

8. Sit down — extinguish the candle.

Halloween
(October 31)

Ingredients

Halloween costume
candles and holders for each person
bouquet of flowers or of colorful fall leaves
drawing paper
crayons
scissors
fireplace or large clay receptacle suitable for burning paper

The ancient Celts believed that each year on November 1, the spirits of the dead returned to mingle with the living. Their ceremonies celebrating All Hallow's Eve, October 31, date back to 700 B.C., when November 1 was considered the beginning of the New Year; thus the Celts not only considered All Hallow's Eve a time of communing with their deceased friends and relatives but also a kind of New Year's celebration.

In a similar vein in the Orient, this is a time for honoring the ancestors. The Shinto tradition includes a ceremony in which a person creates and cuts out paper replicas of the things the deceased loved while on earth. For example, clothes, money, food, jewelry, and favorite animals are some things that could be drawn and painted. In this ritual the loved one now burns these paper symbols believing that this smoke carries the essence of the favorite things to the ancestor in the afterlife.

We will combine both these traditions, the Celtic and the Oriental, in this celebration.

1) Consider October 31 to be New Year's Eve and dress up in a costume that represents the personal quality you'd like to exude in the coming year — kind of a New Year's Eve resolution in tangible form.

2) Everyone sits in a circle, and in the center there is a bouquet of fall flowers or a bouquet of colorful leaves.

3) Each person speaks about the significance of his/her costume and hopes for the New Year, ending with one sentence that succinctly states both of these concepts; for example, "In the New Year I wish to be a butterfly and fly, fly, fly." The group repeats this sentence to the person three times using the individual's name: "In the New Year, Joyce, you will be a butterfly and fly, fly, fly."

4) Each person takes a turn lighting a candle for a deceased friend or relative saying something such like, "I light this candle in memory of my friend Susan who died last year."

5) Each now draws a picture of something the deceased liked and cuts it out. Take the pictures over to the fireplace while the leader lights a fire. As each person places his/her picture in the fireplace, take a moment to speak to the deceased: "George, I send you new clothes for your journey in the spirit world."

6) All sing or recite together this chant from the Self-Realization Fellowship:

> Listen, listen, listen to my heart's song
> Listen, listen, listen to my heart's song
> I will never forget you
> I will never forsake you
> I will never forget you
> I will never forsake you.[1]

NOTES

1. This chant is beautifully sung on the tape/record *Many Blessings* by On the Wings of Song.

Afterword

Feeding the Spirit is primarily about a relationship to nature; however, "nature" in this instance is meant to include more than our usual associations with this word. We are all familiar with nature's outer manifestations (i.e., the sun, moon, and stars as well as the earth with its trees, plants, bodies of water, and its animals). But nature also encompasses many inner aspects. By the word "nature" I also refer to the world of dreams and fantasies, the primitive aspects of our psyche, and the intuitive, instinctual side of our being. This is the realm of the unconscious, a place we don't often explore because we find ourselves so caught up in the conscious world of "making a living." This creative part of each of us, though unconscious, is constantly in touch with the cycles of birth, transformation, and death, which comprise a deeper aspect of our selves. It is this hidden world that I hope to make accessible to people through the exercises in this book.

On a lighter note this book is also about "growing down." From early childhood we strive so long and hard to grow up and act adult that the child in us is often deformed, stifled, or stilted — and so this book can be viewed as a series of prescriptions for play-therapy for adults. When you enter into the spirit of these various exercises, the mind ceases to plague you with questions such as "Is this logical, sensible behavior?" "Will this activity help me get ahead?" "What can I get out of this ritual?" "Am I using my time wisely?" or "What's the outcome of this ceremony?" As the mind quiets and the incessant, internal chatter falls away, you find yourself in a childlike place where play and enjoying each moment is your only goal.

Feeding the Spirit is but a collection of suggestions. Now that you've read through it, be aware that any parts of these exercises can be mixed together in whatever pattern or form you choose. You needn't slavishly adhere to the directions — be creative! Dare to be different: substitute for the ingredients you don't have on hand, delete portions of the exercise that don't appeal to you, and, of course, add creative ideas of your own.

But before you come to any conclusions concerning this book, pick out one recipe and try it. This isn't a book meant to flex your cerebral muscles. It is experiential in its intent, created to bring you closer to the cycles of nature and to your own inner cyclical patterns.

People seem to connect celebrations with food — eating is a way to celebrate holidays, birthdays, anniversaries, and family gatherings. For any special occasion we buy favorite foods, create a feast, or go out to dinner. The recipes within this book create no-calorie, inedible, ceremonial dishes. They present a new twist to the art of celebrating life. Enjoy!

Bibliography

Anderson, Marianne, and Louis Savary. *Passages: A Guide for Pilgrims of the Mind.* New York: Harper & Row, 1972.

Cole, John, and Sara Ebenreck. *Sun Reflections.* Emmans, PA: Rodale Press, 1981.

Gearhart, Sally Miller. *Wanderground.* Boston, MA: Alyson Publications, Inc., 1979.

Guentert, Kenneth, ed. *Winter Festivals.* San Jose, CA: Resource Publications, Inc., 1986.

Gunther, Bernard. *What To Do Till The Messiah Comes,* New York: Collier Book, 1970.

Mestel, Sherry, ed. *Earth Rites.* Vol. 2 of *Rituals.* Brooklyn, NY: Earth Rites Press, 1978.

Rozman, Deborah. *Meditating With Children.* Boulder Creek, CA: University of the Trees Press, 1975.

Starhawk. *The Spiral Dance.* San Francisco, CA: Harper & Row, 1979.

Home Celebration Resources

DANCING CHRISTMAS CAROLS
edited by Doug Adams
Paperbound, $7.95, 135 pages, 5½ " x 8½ "
ISBN 0-89390-006-0
A sourcebook of ideas for carolers of all ages and kinds. The movements presented in the book range from many simple gestures to sophisticated jazz and modern jazz steps.

PASSOVER SEDER FOR CHRISTIAN FAMILIES
Sam Mackintosh
Paperbound, $3.50., Package of 12: $30
31 pages, 5½ " x 8½ "
ISBN 0-89390-057-5
The traditional seder prayers of the Passover meal are presented in a Christian context for celebration at home. Includes complete directions, food recipes, prayers, and an introduction to the seder meal and its Jewish origins. Adaptable for parish use.

TRADITIONALLY YOURS:
Telling the Christian Story Through Family Traditions
Gail Kelley and illustrated by Carol Hershberger
Paperbound, $8.95, 168 pages, 5½ " x 8½ "
ISBN 0-89390-103-2
Learn how to turn everyday events and big family events into family traditions and faith experiences. The personal accounts in this book are a springboard for establishing your own traditions, which can in turn help you establish Christian values, attitudes, and love within your family.

LEARNING TO LIVE TOGETHER:
At Home and in the World
Jacqueline Haessly
Paperbound, $6.95, 87 pages, 5½ " x 8½ "
ISBN 0-89390-121-0
Both idealistic and practical, this book gives insight and information as well as activities to help the family actually become peacemakers. Topics include affirmation, communication, values, respect for differences, cooperation, and conflict resolution. Formerly titled *Peacemaking: Family Activities for Justice and Peace.*

SEASONAL STORIES FOR FAMILY FESTIVALS
Armandine Kelly
Paperbound, $7.95, 128 pages, 5½ " x 8½ "
ISBN 0-89390-096-6
Discover the trditions behind some of your favorite holidays and feast days, plus learn about some not-so-well-known celebrations. Includes creative suggestions for celebrating each holiday and feast day.

Resources for Spiritual Growth

PRAYER WORDS: An Exercise in Meditative Prayer
Graham Smith
Paperbound, $10.95, 120 pages, 5 ½ " x 8 ½ " ISBN 0-89390-187-3
Here is a practical manual on mysticism that you can use in your own life or in small groups. Graham Smith outlines a simple meditation technique, using 60 sacred words from various religious traditions. Latin. Sanskrit. Hebrew. Greek. English. Using each word in your meditation practice integrates body and soul, male and female, and the conscious and unconscious. This book offers a fresh angle: the integration of Christian and non-Christian spirituality within the context of prayer.

WINNING YOUR INNER BATTLE
Including Guided Imagery Meditations
Jeanne Heiberg
Paperbound, $8.95, 152 pages, 5 ½ " x 8 ½ " ISBN 0-89390-159-8
Life is full of external dangers and problems. However, the greater battleground is with your own thoughts, feelings, and attitudes. The author, based on her personal experiences, shows you how to win the inner battle by taming your internal dragons and turning them into allies for life's journey. Each chapter ends with a guided imagery meditation that you can use by yourself or in a group.

THE DEBRIS OF THR ENCOUNTER
A Recovery of Self
Terre Ouwehand
Paperbound, $7.95, 78 pages, 5 ½ " x 8 ½ " ISBN 0-89390-137-7
During a period of psychotherapeutic exploration, Terre Ouwehand began meditating and experienced what psychologists call eidetic imagery or what mystics call inner visions. *The Debris of the Encounter* is her story of recovery and healing. Ouwehand, a gifted playwright, works with bold images to convey an unfolding sense of a higher power at work in her life.

FINDING THE CLOWN IN YOURSELF:
Personal Growth for Every Christian
Jack Krall and Jan Kalberer
Paperbound, $8.95, 102 pages, 5 ½ " x 8 ½ " ISBN 0-89390-179-2
Two active clowns show you how to develop your own spirituality by first finding "the little clown" in yourself. Each chapter ends with a Scripture reflection, questions for self-examination, and suggestions for further reflection.

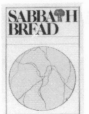

SABBATH BREAD: For Personal Sacred-Searching and
Group Faith-Sharing
Georgene Wilson
Paperbound, $9.95, 145 pages, 5 ½ " x 8 ½ " ISBN 0-89390-101-6
In *Sabbath Bread*, you'll find a wealth of new ideas and techniques for your Christian faith-sharing group. Using the reflections, stories, and prayers, you'll suddenly see the sacred in the ordinary and be able to help your friends see it too! Includes outlines of three community retreats.

Performing Arts

STORYTELLING STEP BY STEP
Marsh Cassady
Paperbound, $9.95, 140 pages, 5½" x 8½"
ISBN 0-89390-183-0
If you tell stories for any reason — or want to — this is the book for you. Marsh Cassady, a storyteller and drama instructor, takes you through all the necessary steps: selecting the right story for you, selecting the right story for your audience, adapting your story for different occasions, analyzing it so that you can present it well, preparing your audience, and presenting the story. Along the way, he includes many examples of stories that work.

ACTING STEP BY STEP
Marsh Cassady
Paperbound, $9.95, 186 pages, 5½" x 8½"
ISBN 0-89390-120-2
People involved in person-to-person activities should have a basic knowledge of acting in order to have an effect on the audience. *Acting Step by Step* trains the beginner to find a workable presentation of body movement and voice, technique and script, improvisation, rehearsal, and finally, performance.

PLAYWRITING STEP BY STEP
Marsh Cassady
Paperbound, $8.95, 148 pages, 5½" x 8½"
ISBN 0-89390-056-7
Whether you write three-act plays or five-minute skits, you'll want this handy how-to book. Covers the six elements of good drama: plot, thought, character, diction, melody, and spectacle. An excellent reference.

DIRECTING PUPPET THEATRE STEP BY STEP
Carol Fijan and Frank Ballard
Paperbound, $14.95, 96 pages, 7" x 10"
ISBN 0-89390-126-1
This book can give you the information you need to be successful at puppet theatre. You will learn the principles of directing and how to apply them to puppet groups of all sizes and shapes. The authors present their information clearly and simply so you may easily put them into practice. Includes complete script and blocking of *Where Are You, Cinderella?*.

Working with Teenagers?